AF381455

BOOK ANALYSIS

Written by Chloé De Smet
Translated by Rebecca Neal

Based on a True Story

BY DELPHINE DE VIGAN

BOOK ANALYSIS

Shed new light
on your favorite books with

Bright
Summaries.com

www.brightsummaries.com

DELPHINE DE VIGAN

- **Born in Boulogne-Billancourt (France) in 1966.**
- **Notable works:**
  - *No and Me* (2007), novel
  - *Underground Time* (2009), novel
  - *Nothing Holds Back the Night* (2011), novel

Delphine de Vigan is a French author who has achieved considerable literary success in recent years, in particular thanks to her novels *No and Me* (which won France's Prix des libraires in 2008) and *Underground Time*, as well as her autobiographical book *Nothing Holds Back the Night* (which won the Prix Renaudot young adult, the prix du roman Fnac and the Grand prix des lectrices de Elle in 2011). The boundary between fiction and reality is somewhat blurred in her books, and her warm, fluid writing provides readers with a glimpse of her inner self. However, de Vigan remains modest and reserved and has little taste for the media exposure that has accompanied her professional success. In addition to her career as a novelist, she also has a passion for film: several of her novels have been adapted for the cinema, and in 2014 she directed her first feature-length film, *À coup sûr.*

BASED ON A TRUE STORY

A WAY OF WRITING ABOUT THE SELF

- **Genre:** autobiography, thriller
- **Reference edition:** De Vigan, D. (2017) *Based on a True Story*. Trans. Miller, G. London: Bloomsbury.
- **1st edition:** 2015
- **Themes:** manipulation, fiction, reality, doubles, seduction, depression, duality

Based on a True Story is Delphine de Vigan's eighth novel and was an immediate hit when it was published in 2015. It was nominated for the Prix Goncourt, Prix Renaudot and Prix Médicis, three of France's most prestigious literary awards, in 2015, and also proved very popular with readers. This novel, which lies somewhere between autobiography and thriller, tells the story of an ambiguous friendship between Delphine, the narrator, and a woman known only as "L.", whom she meets by chance and who begins to encroach more and more on her life. Within this novel,

which has many of the features of a psychological thriller, the author raises questions about the
duality of the writer and the legitimacy of fiction
within literature.

SUMMARY

AN AUTHOR SUFFERING FROM WRITER'S BLOCK

The novel's narrator, Delphine, is a successful author but is beset by doubts as she finds herself at a loss for inspiration. She then gives a retrospective account of the events preceding her writer's block and the role her new friend L. has played in her painful, frustrating situation.

As well as her writing struggles, Delphine has been isolating herself over the course of the previous days and weeks. She has stopped paying her bills and answering her emails, and no longer sees anybody apart from L. This means that she no longer has a social life and has sunk into a deep depression. One day, she tries to start writing again by imagining a purely fictional reality television show character, then by going back to one of her unfinished books, but to no avail. She cannot write a single line, and even sitting in front of her computer makes her feel sick.

When L. moves into the protagonist's apartment, Delphine lets herself go even more, wandering aimlessly and not doing anything productive. This unknown woman seems to take pleasure in taking care of her friend and insists that she get back to writing, although she does not leave her much freedom. L. acts as though she is the only person who truly knows Delphine and can judge her potential as a writer. Weeks go by and the situation remains unchanged: L. covers for her friend's inactivity by taking charge of her mail, her bills and some of her other projects. She even cowrites the preface for a new edition of a text by Maupassant (French writer, 1850-1893) that Delphine was supposed to write. But how did it come to this? Where do Delphine's problems come from?

HER MEETING WITH L.

Delphine meets L. at a drinks reception. From their very first conversation, it is clear that they have a number of things in common: they are both authors, they both enjoy the cinema, they are both independent, they are both curious about other people, and so on. A friendship blossoms between them. Delphine, who has been feeling tense and exhausted since her last book came out, soon finds that confiding in her friend feels natural. She is naturally shy, so she does not like being the centre of attention and struggles with her fame. Furthermore, her recent success worries her: will she manage to do better with her next novel? And what if this book turns out to be her last one? She tells L. about how she feels. The other woman is very receptive to her and seems to be the person who is best placed to listen to her and understand her feelings, even though they only met a few hours ago.

After this evening, the two women maintain an all-consuming friendship, seeing each other every day and regularly talking on the phone. At the same time, Delphine starts receiving anonymous threatening letters which seem to come from a family member or someone close to her. These letters have a powerful effect on her and push her a little further into her life of apathy. In addition, Delphine starts remembering flashes of her past and realises that she has already met L., as they were at school together. But why has L. never mentioned this? Was their meeting at the drinks reception really a chance encounter? Delphine is afraid of where these questions could lead, so she keeps them to herself.

BETWEEN FICTION AND REALITY

The relationship between the two women takes a new turn when Delphine starts to become more independent and agrees to an interview with a journalist who wants to talk to her about one of her novels. During this interview, the narrator enjoys telling her story and talking to someone other than L. Furthermore, Delphine refuses to write another autobiographical book, but L. has her heart set on this and insists that she has to do it. Apart from this difference of opinion, the two women live peacefully together. However, Delphine's inability to write is a shared secret that creates a dangerous bond between them, particularly when L. replaces the heroine when she can no longer avoid writing and becomes her ghostwriter.

However, one day Delphine finds out that L. has secretly sent an email to all her friends telling them not to contact her any more, and the two women have a blazing row. L. tries to justify her actions by explaining that the narrator needs to concentrate on writing her next novel. The day after this altercation, L. leaves Delphine's apartment and moves into a hotel. However, before long chance throws the women back together when Delphine mysteriously falls down the stairs in her apartment. Her so-called friend just happens to be nearby and rushes to her aid. Now that her leg is in a splint and she has to use crutches, the narrator finds it difficult to live alone. Her partner François, a literary critic, is abroad for work, so he cannot look after her. Naturally, L. offers to take care of Delphine, and the two women hole up in François' house in Courseilles, Normandy, so that the writer can get back to focusing on her next book.

During this trip, the two women find themselves behind closed doors and completely sealed off from the world. For the first time since they met, L. confides in Delphine, telling her about her husband's suicide and her difficult childhood. But is she telling the truth? Although the narrator initially believes her, afterwards she has major doubts. The days go by and Delphine has a sudden revelation: L. will be the subject of her next novel. As she is afraid of the other woman's reaction, she keeps the plot of the story to herself. Unfortunately, she thinks that L. has worked out what she is planning to do, although she does not know for certain. At the same time, the heroine becomes so ill that she can no longer get out of bed. This time, she does not think it can just be a coincidence, and is convinced that her so-called friend is poisoning her. Then, every-thing happens very quickly: she runs away, faints and is hospitalised.

Delphine wakes up in a hospital bed with François next to her. She tells him everything, from her meeting with L. up to her present situa-tion. However, her story seems far-fetched, and even her partner has trouble believing it. Indeed, it seems that nobody knows L., or has even met her. Furthermore, there is no sign that anyone apart from Delphine was living at Courseilles.

If L. has vanished from her life for good, the writer still has one final question: did she really exist? One day, Delphine receives a phone call from her editor, who congratulates her on her brilliant new book. The narrator is stunned and dismayed because she has not written anything for months, and realises that L. has taken her name and has written a book that will be more successful than anything she could have written. Fiction or reality? Madness or reason? Deception or betrayal? At the end of the narrative, doubts remain with regard to the identity of the author of the novel, and to the very existence of L.

CHARACTER STUDY

DELPHINE

Delphine, the book's narrator, is a novelist in her forties who lives in Paris. She is a divorced mother of two and is in a relationship with François, although she lives alone. Since the publication of her last novel, she has been struggling with her sudden fame (invitations to bookshops and schools, interview requests from journalists, and so on). As she is naturally shy and emotional, Delphine finds her new popularity difficult to deal with: she cannot stand being the centre of attention and feels helpless in front of her readers and the press. The book that brought her this dazzling success is about a very personal part of her life. She explains: "I'd written a book whose impact I hadn't foreseen." Consequently, she feels the need to keep some distance from her readers.

Furthermore, the narrator is an independent woman who likes doing things alone, although she also enjoys being with her friends. She does not feel at all at ease in large groups, but cherishes more intimate relationships. In addition, she is very quick to make friends and remains loyal to people she likes: "It's undeniable that I'm someone who forms attachments, and attachments that last."

When she meets L., Delphine has just come from a book fair where she felt too weak to sign her book. Even though she is feeling fragile, tense and exhausted, she still goes to the drinks reception where L. approaches her – or was it the other way round? Whatever the case, when the two women meet, Delphine is positioned as the victim and L. plays the role of her saviour.

The resemblance between the two characters in undeniable: they are both independent writers who live alone in apartments in Paris. Solitude is one of the most important things they have in common. For Delphine, this isolation results from a series of departures that have had a major impact on her life: her children have flown the nest, her friends have moved to the country and François travels regularly. Because they are so similar, the narrator quickly becomes attached to L. More than just friendship, an unshakeable

bond and an unhealthy mutual fascination deve-
lop between the two women. Delphine feels that
her friend has all the qualities that she wishes she
had (self-confidence, charisma, elegance, and so
on). She admires her for this and, above all, for
her ability to write when she herself is suffering
from writer's block.

L.

The initial L., which first appears in the opening
pages of the novel, refers to a female character
in her forties living in Paris. L., whose name we
are never told, was a journalist before working
as a ghostwriter for women's autobiographies.
Throughout the novel, she is always described
through Delphine's eyes:

> "L. was perfect. She made me think of Gérard
> Darel ads. I remember it clearly: precisely that
> – the simple, modern sophistication, the skilful
> mix of classic, conservative materials and bold
> details."

As we can see, the narrator views L. as a very
beautiful, elegant woman who turns men's
heads. In addition, she seems very attentive and

empathetic: "I realised quite quickly that L. had an incredible sense of the Other, a gift for saying the right thing, telling people exactly what they needed to hear."

In spite of her apparent composure and emotional availability, L. seems to be carrying a burden from her past that she is unable to talk about: "Something in her, something buried and barely perceptible, suggested that L. had come back from far away". Her husband committed suicide a few years ago, leaving her widowed and childless. Since then, she has been living alone and has lost touch with most of her friends. Her personality is paradoxical: on the one hand, she seems poised and controlled, but on the other hand she can be unpredictable and violent. In this way, we see her in different lights: sometimes funny and cheerful, at other times sensitive and mysterious. Besides this contradictory temperament, L. has some phobias (for example, she is morbidly afraid of rodents) and carries out strange rituals when she eats out or invites someone over. Consequently, the different facets of her personality sow doubt in the mind of the reader, who is unsure what to make of this enigmatic character.

FRANÇOIS

François is a literary critic and has been Delphine's partner for several years. He often has to travel abroad for work. The narrator describes him as "[t]he man I love". In spite of the bond between them, François is not very present in Delphine's life. He is very busy and has a number of responsibilities, and seems to prefer it if each half of the couple maintains their independence and privacy.

When the narrator starts spending time with L., she does not say anything to François about her, and he never meets her. Furthermore, Delphine does not dare to tell François about her writing struggles. Since he has an intimate knowledge of the literary world, she is scared that he will judge her, or worse, stop loving her. When Delphine comes back from Courseilles, François does not trust her version of events, as he deems it improbable. He believes that L. is nothing more than a figment of the narrator's imagination, a sort of double of herself who serves as a pretext to write another book.

ANALYSIS

A SORT OF AUTOBIOGRAPHY

Based on a True Story could be considered as a kind of autobiographical text, as it contains many of the characteristics of this genre. Firstly, the narrator tells her story in the first person. Secondly, there are some personal elements from de Vigan's own life: her first name, the fact that she is a writer, the fact that she is divorced and has two children, her shyness, her struggles with fame, the success of her last book, the fact that her partner is a literary critic, and so on. Everything is subtly set out to give us the impression that the book is autobiographical.

However, some elements make the novel different from traditional autobiographical writing. First of all, there is the presence of L., the new friend who appears out of nowhere and whom the reader constantly wonders about. Is she real? Or was she created by the writer (the narrator of the novel) as a plot device for her next book? Doubt lingers. In addition, the central subject of de Vigan's novel remains vague: is this really a story of manipulation and betrayal by a friend? Or does it have another meaning? In fact, could this plot be a pretext to express the author's unease at her celebrity and her fear of writing her next book? These fictional and vague elements make the novel different from autobiography as we usually conceive of it.

Based on a True Story is also set apart from pure autobiography by its close link with the psychological thriller. This literary genre is a subgenre of the thriller and the horror novel, and focuses on the mental and emotional conflict experienced by the characters. For example, they often experience hallucinations and paranoia. In *Based on a True Story*, we can see the characteristics of this genre in Delphine's emotional disturbance: on multiple occasions, we find ourselves unsure about her lucidity and her mental health. Furthermore, the reader is kept on tenterhooks throughout the book, like in a detective novel. We wonder constantly about L.'s true identity and what is going to happen next. We feel that something big is about to happen, and this proves to be the case, as L. tries to poison Delphine at the end of the story. Finally, explicit references to the American writer and master of suspense Stephen King (born in 1947) are used as epigraphs at the start of each section: "'Inside him a voice whispered for the first time: Who are you when you write, Thad? Who are you then?' Stephen King, *The Dark Half*". Specifically, *Based on a True Story* seems to be directly inspired by the King novel *Misery* (1987), in which a successful writer is kidnapped by one of his admirers. These quotations ratchet up the tension, and the shadow of King only increases the reader's anxiety.

THE DUALITY OF THE WRITER

At one point in the novel, François says that he feels like there are times when someone takes possession of Delphine, in this way foregrounding the theme of duality. As we progress through the novel, we become aware that it is not just about manipulation and betrayal. Indeed, the novel invites us to reflect on the duality of human beings, and more specifically on the duality of writers.

The mysterious, somewhat controlling relationship between the two women raises questions about doubles, and leaves us wondering whether we might all be made up of two contrasting sides. Does this only apply to writers, or is it true of all human beings? When they write, authors seem to have two personalities that both oppose and complement each other: their personality in real life, and the personality that they embody in their novels, which differs from their true self and which may compensate for their own flaws. The duality of the writer can be seen in the characters of Delphine and L.: they resemble and complement one another, and one woman's assets make up for the other's failings. For example, L. has social and interpersonal skills that the writer can only dream of. She seems like an improved version of Delphine. Throughout the novel, we have the impression that L. is gradually replacing the narrator, until the two women are one and the same person.

As such, at the end of the novel, the reader wonders whether the two protagonists could represent the two sides of a single person, like yin and yang. Seen from this angle, Delphine could have a confident side that gets whatever it wants, represented through L., and another, introverted side that struggles to reach its goals.

THE STATUS OF FICTION WITHIN LITERATURE

Based on a True Story also raises questions about the act of writing, though the unease that Delphine feels when she is unable to write her next book. In this context, the book deals with the status of fiction within literature. Indeed, it features multiple long conversations between L. and Delphine, who have different views on this controversial subject: should literary works be entirely fictional? Or, conversely, is autobiography the only thing worth writing? What is the meaning of writing? According to L., "nothing remains of fictional characters who have no link with reality." She is convinced that "[t]he only sort of writing is writing about the self." In addition, she thinks that people no longer believe in fiction and are looking for truth: for a novel to be worthwhile, it absolutely must refer to reality, or it risks being seen as empty and impersonal. Consequently, L. insists that Delphine should write a book based on her own experiences, without relying on fiction. Conversely, Delphine thinks that the important thing in a novel is that it allows the reader to escape, lose them- selves in the story and be entertained. She is convinced that this is why literature exists and, consequently, that it is essential to incorporate fictional elements.

FURTHER REFLECTION

- "[A]ny writing about the self is a novel. [Story] is an illusion. It doesn't exist. No book should be authorised to have that printed on its cover." Comment on this quote.
- In your opinion, to what extent does *Based on a True Story* contain an autobiographical dimension? Justify your answer using examples from the text.
- Explain the three phases of the novel: seduction, depression and betrayal.
- In your opinion, is L. a real person or a figment of Delphine's imagination? Justify your answer.
- In light of the theme of doubles, how would you interpret the following quote: "Today I know that L. is the sole reason for my powerlessness"?
- In your opinion, at a time when real-life stories, documentary narratives and other personal accounts are meeting with great success,

what place can we reserve for fiction within literature?
- How does the novel generate suspense?
- "The reader was always up for yielding and treating fiction like reality." Do you agree with this quotation from the author?
- Several of Delphine de Vigan's books have already been adapted for the cinema. In your opinion, would it be possible to do the same with this book? If so, how would you go about it?
- Using extracts from the text to support your answer, explain the narrator's feeling of duality.

We want to hear from you!
Leave a comment on your online library
and share your favourite books on social media!

FURTHER READING

REFERENCE EDITION

- De Vigan, D. (2017) *Based on a True Story*. Trans. Miller, G. London: Bloomsbury.

MORE FROM BRIGHTSUMMARIES. COM

- Reading guide – *No and Me* by Delphine de Vigan.
- Reading guide – *Nothing Holds Back the Night* by Delphine de Vigan.
- Reading guide – *Underground Time* by Delphine de Vigan.

BOOK ANALYSIS

Bright
≣Summaries.com

More guides to rediscover your love of literature

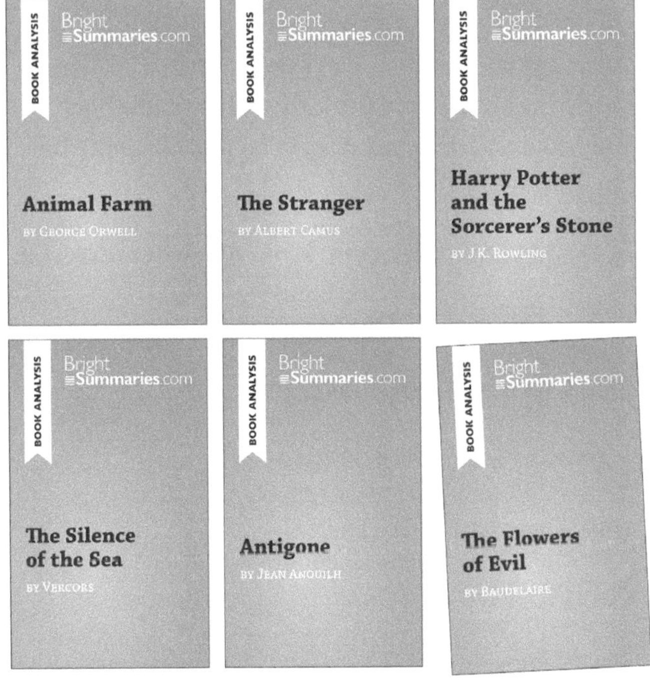

www.brightsummaries.com

Although the editor makes every effort to verify the accuracy of the information published, BrightSummaries.com accepts no responsibility for the content of this book.

© **BrightSummaries.com, 2016. All rights reserved.**

www.brightsummaries.com

Ebook EAN: 9782808004442

Paperback EAN: 9782808004459

Legal Deposit: D/2017/12603/752

Cover: © Primento

Digital conception by Primento, the digital partner of publishers.